Maria: The Life Story of a World War II Italian Bride

Maria: The Life Story of a World War II Italian Bride

Maria Leonardi-Lamorte

iUniverse, Inc.
New York Lincoln Shanghai

Maria: The Life Story of a World War II Italian Bride

iUniverse books may be ordered through booksellers or by contacting:

iUniverse
2021 Pine Lake Road, Suite 100
Lincoln, NE 68512
www.iuniverse.com
1-800-Authors (1-800-288-4677)

The views expressed in this work are solely those of the author and do not necessarily reflect the views of the publisher, and the publisher hereby disclaims any responsibility for them.

ISBN-13: 978-0-595-42289-0 (pbk)
ISBN-13: 978-0-595-86626-7 (ebk)
ISBN-10: 0-595-42289-6 (pbk)
ISBN-10: 0-595-86626-3 (ebk)

Printed in the United States of America

I dedicate this book to my family.
I want to let them know about my
Belief in and my love for God.
He is my strength and my inspiration.
I was blessed to write this book of my
Life, here in this country that I love.

When I was born,
I was a unique creation of god.
He made me one of a kind and, by
Putting my trust in him,
I became one of God's masterpieces,
Which made me very special.
And he's the one who made it possible.
Also I want the world to know about
His great love and tender mercy.

Contents

1

In the beginning

I was born on the forth of February, 1923, in Naples on the coast of Italy. The address was number 54 Via Firenze. Present at the event were two neighbors, my Aunt Michela, and the midwife. As I emerged into the world, the midwife exclaimed "It's a girl, born with a caul. The woman, being much moved, said that the baby was born lucky and her life would be full of joy. They baptized me "Maria".

My Family consisted of my father, Luigi Leonardo, my mother Anna Amodeo, my brother Salvatore, and me. Two years later another member of the family was born, a beautiful baby boy with blue eye and golden curls and my parents called him Franchesco.

When he was two years old, Franchesco became very ill with measles and then pneumonia. Although I had also contracted measles, I stayed active and did not stay in bed. The Doctor said if Francesco did recover he would be blind for the rest of his life. However, his destiny was not of this world, the Lord called him. As time went by the baby appeared in a dream to a friend of the family and said, "I was giving my place to my sister, Maria."

I grew up care-free and happy. I was good-natured and always had a smile for everyone. I was into everything so they nicknamed me, "Vespa—the Bee." I was gregarious and well liked by everybody including the nuns at the kindergarten that I attended later.

Looking back, I vaguely remember my parents especially my father, who was a engineer and worked for the railroad. He was born in Naples on June 28th, 1890. Because he worked for the government, we had a little private home which was given to us through his job.

My father traveled to a lot of places like Salerno, Cassino, Rome, and Villa Literno, sometimes for a few days at a time. When he returned home to Naples, he would never come empty handed. From farms he passed in his train he would bring farm foods like eggs. He would also bring candies and cookies for me and my brother. Sometimes, my mother would take my brother and me to the station to wait for my father. Whenever I heard the train whistle, it would bring back happy memories of my father picking up my brother and I, lifting us happily into the air and covering us with kisses. These memories will always be precious to me and I will not forget them. I still dream of those whistles and of the love long ago. How many times I think of that train.

My father and I were inseparable. I remember him as a very religious and charitable man. Although he led a difficult life, filled with limitations and hardships, he loved nature and every living creature with all his heart. He would give the pigeon's food and money to people begging on the street. He believed in the truth. He often talked to my brother and I about being good and respecting and loving each other and every living creature.

My father taught me how to swim. He also licked to cook special dinners, such as pasta sauces, omelets and frittata. During the week he would take us to church and after Mass, we would go into the crypt and visit the catacombs. This was a place where they kept skeletons and sculls surrounded by candles. My brothers and I were scared but my dad made us touch the sculls so that we would overcome the fright of seeing them.

In the 1930's, when I was seven, I vaguely remember an earthquake. During the night we woke feeling the earth shaking. Everyone was frightened and I was terribly upset and could hardly understand what all the excitement was about, but thanks to God it only lasted a few seconds.

When I was 9 years old, I hurt myself by falling down on steps made of marble, while dressed in my mom's high heels. I banged my head on the hard stone and passed out. I was taken to the hospital and remained in a coma with no sign of life for three days. I did not recognize anyone because of the brain injury, I could have died instantly but was very fortunate that the Lord was always near me and protected me from all my mischief.

2

My Parents

My mother came from a wealthy family. Her father, Michelle Amodeo, born in Monte forte in the province of Avellino near Naples, inherited land with olive trees and vineyards. He was always busy, but decided to make time to get away for a vacation and took a trip to France. He stayed there for a while and went to Marseille where he meets a girl, her name was Sharaten Marchepet. He got to know her well and falls in love. However, his vacation time was getting short and he had to return home. He did not want to leave her behind so they decided to get married and then he brought her back to Italy as his wife.

After some time she became pregnant and gave birth to a little girl, who was my mother, Anna Amodeo. During the birth of her second child she lost her life, leaving behind another daughter, my Aunt Michela. She was so young, only 33 years old. The girls both grew up without the love of their mother, but at first they had a governess who took care of them. Later, the girls were separated but they were well taken care of. Although my mother was the first born she grew up very scared of life and afraid to do anything herself.

The day came when she met the man of her dreams who was to become my father. He was handsome and good natured. Btu soon after they married she became jealous and suspicious because she was insecure, which led them to fight between themselves. I remember as a little girl my dad would be a little rough with my mother, he would push her and tell her off. I did not like this, but I knew my dad had a good heart. He had a great love for God and a deep faith. He received a multitude of miracle, such as dreams, in which the future and certain events were reveled to him. He dedicated his life to the Lord and made many sacrifices. I remember this like it was yesterday. My mom was sometimes bitter and serious and she rarely smiled. My dad believed you should live each day and not worry about tomorrow. Live and let live. My mother had different ideas such as we should save for tomorrow.

My father's sister, Fortuna had a bad marriage. She married a man named Paolo Zamputo who was not good for her. He looked like Rudolph Valentino, the actor from Sicily. He was a tough character, he worked as a security guard and did his job making sure that know one got away with anything. He made a whip out of horse tail and used it to do things his way. Because of his job he was out of town a lot. One time in Africa he contracted syphilis, which unfortunately was passed to his wife, my aunt. Although she was alright she gave birth to a baby girl, who fully developed but never grew tall and was simple—minded.

When I visited the family, the daughter Nanninella liked me a lot because I would pay attention to her by cooking her breakfast and watching out for her. While she was young her father died. Then as time passed, the small Nanninella fell asleep one day, never again to wake up. I remember how sad that was for me.

Many times, while sitting on my fathers lap, I could not help noticing the tears coming down his cheeks. I would ask why he was so sad. As he cried, I would often hear a song on the phonograph he would play. The song was titled, "Tell her I love her." He would reply that the song reminded him of his younger sister Assunta, who had committed suicide at a young age. She had felt that suicide was her only option of escaping the pain of vicious gossip that had prematurely ended her romance with the young fellow that she loved. When her mother had told her that the neighbors were talking about the young couple, Assunta have run out to a local store and bought some lye, commonly used in lawn trees in those days. She swallowed a couple and passed away three months after unbelievable suffering. It was a very tragic and heartbreaking time for the families involved. The young couple had been completely in love and was constantly being compared to "Romeo and Juliet." Assunta was a beautiful girl and her lost innocence and hope was a terrible consequence and an extreme loss for all.

As my father and I continued to talk, he went on to tell me about his father, my grandfather, Francesco Leonardi, who looked like Frank Sinatra. He worked as a horse and buggy driver. At age 74 he died from brain thrombosis. He was very different from his son; he had a bid of a perverted mind.

My father's mother's name was Carmela Russo. She suffered from a severely debilitating case of arthritis, which caused her to shrink in stature and eventually pass away before she was an old woman. I love to listen to my dad as he would tell me the family stories. The stories however, were sad and it was painful to hear of all the awful things that happened throughout my family's many generations. I knew that one day I would be able to tell my children stories about their Italian relatives.

As I continue to write the family adventure, I will pick up the story on my mother's side, with her sister, my aunt Michela, who married a first cousin, John. It is well known that during between blood relatives is dangerous, but being in love as they were, they were willing to take the chance and they did. They took their vows and had three children to boys and one girl, Salvatore, Geraldo and Chiarraina. Luckily all these children were normal and Salvatore became a Catholic priest. Then, later on, my aunts had another child. It seemed to be normal, but as it grew older, they discovered it had a hunched back. He unfortunately died at an early age.

My Uncle John and on Michela lived in the country. He was a journalist, who printed the local newspaper. He was funny and was happy-go-lucky. During summer vacations, my brother and I would stay with them on the farm. The sounds of the rooster and the birds singing in early morning and the dogs barking would wake me up very early. We would drink fresh milk from the cow. The fresh air and the beauty surrounding us was refreshing.

3

My Growing Up Years

I started school at Lugi Miraghia elementary school, not far from home. My teacher's name was Maione and she taught us a little bit of everything. As I walked home from school, I would admire the good and bad, especially the creations of God in nature. Sometimes the rough winds and heavy rains would fill the streets up, making it very difficult to cross the streets. Local authorities would boards up that we would use to cross over to the other side of the street. On sunny days, we would lie on the grass and enjoy the radiant sun going through me. I used to like to pick up the daisies in the field and loved juggling balls in the air. I could even double three or four balls in one hand. I also enjoyed jumping rope. The best of all, I'd love to make believe that I was really cooking with my mother. She would make a small fire for us outside and we would cook over it.

By this time, we were under the government leader, fascist Benito Mussolini. he was a man of great power. One time I saw him when he spoke to the people from the balcony of an official building in Rome. His voice was very powerful; we were scared it sounded earthshaking, like an earthquake I had experienced earlier. However, he built schools with gymnasiums so we could participate in gymnastics, which I loved. I remember wearing a black skirt and white blouse to gym class.

My schooling was completed in the fifth grade. This was because my family thought education for a girl was not very important. A boy's education was considered very important since he would have the responsibility of one day supporting a wife and family. I'm happy that even though I was finished with schooling at such a young age, I did receive a diploma for the time I attended school.

I have always loved to read and hope to become somebody important in my life, my big dream was to become an actress. My passion was music critically opera such as La Boheme, Madame Butterfly and Tosca. I also loved popular music. My favorite songs were "Blue Moon", "Pallida Luna" in Italian, "I walk alone" and "I'll be seeing you" sung by Vera Lynn during World War II.

Since I appeared older than my years due to my early physical development, I hope that someday I could come to America. Perhaps my dream would become a reality. Although I had to put my dreams on hold and I was still young, I could recall my mother being sad because of a tragedy that happened to my dad. My dad was at work checking a problem with a wire on top of the train. In the meantime his colleague did not know that my dad was up there and started to move the train. This caused my poor Dad to fall off the train, landing on the track on his back. He yelled for help and was taken to hospital. He had injured his spine and was in much pain.

He remained out of work for six months and recovered very slowly, becoming very depressed during this time. The railroad company gave him a very small pension, which was not enough to live on. This made my mother scared, and since we could not manage she was in a panic. She decided to call a lawyer to sue the state. But nothing was settled. So we had to leave the house we were living in, which belong to the state and go elsewhere to a miserable apartment. Thanks to the faith in God that we had, my dad did eventually recover and got another job as an administrator, but he worked hard for the family so that we could survive.

That was my turn to pitch in and I decided that I would like to become a seamstress. I felt it was important to learn different things and knew that sewing would become important for me at a later time in my life, what I would have my own family sew for.

Time marches on and when I was about 18 years old, I met two sisters, Maria and Helen. Maria was married to a mechanic but Helen was single. Helen and I became very close friends. Marie's husband had a vespa motorcycle. He taught me how to ride it, which was a lot of fun and exciting. Helen and I enjoyed going out together on Saturday nights to a club, called Orange Gardens. We would meet boys there and go dancing. I will never forget a story she told me one evening while we were there, it made such an impression on my mind. She told me the story of what happened to her. Several years before, she had been engaged to a very good-looking guy, but he was very jealous. One night they were going out and he became angry at her. Helen did not tell me exactly why he was angry, but that he grabbed her in an alley and in a fit of rage took a razor and slashed her face from the top of her eyes to the bottom of her mouth. She was scarred for life. I realize now why she wore her long blond hair like Veronica Lake. What a terrible shame. She was a beautiful girl. After the war we lost contact with each other and I'm still trying to find her.

My brother Salvatore and I were like twins. We always spent a lot of time together. He had always been interested in joining a seminary, but this never materialized. He did however complete his college education. I also want to mention how he was very athletic. He love to ski, plays soccer, and baseball. My brother was very strong. This I feel is perhaps due to the fact that he was dipped in wine after his birth. Salvatore, who was very handsome, was considered by those who knew him to look a lot like Robert Taylor. He was a very kind and generous person and had many good friends, who were always at our home playing card games. I used to serve them espresso coffee and goodies.

Among Salvatore's friends was one in whom I became interested. This was Domenico Leone, who became my first love. We dated and then we became serious about our courtship. My father and mother knew how we felt about each other and that marriage was in our minds. We became engaged and my father, who had a lot of influence, got Domenico a state job.

As time went on, my brother Salvatore got drafted into the air force, where he became a specialized mechanic, while Domenico was drafted into the Marines and had to leave home. He was away for some time before arriving back home for leave. When I saw him in his uniform, I felt that he become very self important, at least he gave me the impression that he felt very superior to everyone around him. I now felt that we have lost the magic feeling we once had for each other.

4

World War II Starts

In 1941, World War II broke out, which tried to continue our family life style as we were accustomed to. We were a plain and religious family, closest to God and always attended Mass on Sundays. We're a very devoted family, my daddy made sure we always had a little wine and bread on our dinner table. This reminded us of the body and blood of Christ. Our family was close, and we would sit around our home on the cold and windy days, near the furnace on the floor. he also would tell us about religious stories and he also served the mass with my cousin, Padre Salerno Salvatore.

Times became very difficult. Money and food were scarce. Germany invaded Italy and took control of everything. They came in to Naples and tanks and trucks and the Nazis took over the city. Some of German soldiers were nice. One of them supplied our family with food and begged me to take him to church because he wanted to pray to God. He was very sympathetic. Others were not so good and would threaten to kill us. They would say"caput" meaning, I will kill you. It was very terrifying for everyone.

One day, on my way to the store, traveling with the bus I had to go through an area that was bombed and two German soldiers approached and I felt a rifle on my neck. I naturally fell they were going to kill me and I was terrified and ran away. This happened more than once. I believe that God was right there at that moment and I was saved. I know in my heart this was truly a miracle.

We had to wait in long lines at 5:00 a.m. for food which was rationed. Sometimes, by the time we reached the front of the line, everything would be gone and there would be nothing to eat. The Medusa restaurant, which was near a corner where we lived, often gave me food. However, I would think of my parents at home who needed the food more than I did. I felt I could share with them, since

I was much younger, I would do anything for my parents. Many times we were starving and had to eat grass.

I'll never forget the times we had to stay in our bomb shelter when the bombs were coming. My dad suggested that the people in our building go through our apartment to get to the bomb shelter, instead of going outside the building. He felt that it would be quicker and safer since everyone was frightened and running like crazy to take cover. My father had made a large, beautiful crucifix that the people pass by on their way to the shelter and this helped them keep their faith and gave him courage.

We sometimes stayed all night and many times into the next day before we could go back to our first floor. We would be forced to wear gas masks, bend our bodies' foreword and put our heads to the floor. We had to try to protect ourselves in this manner. Everything was a blackout. People could go outside only in groups of four with a small searchlight.

One time, our entire family was trapped in the bomb shelter. The firemen had to dig all around outside where the bombs did all the damage. We all prayed on our knees and when it was all over, we were saved. The surroundings outside were a mess. There was water everywhere. It had been like an inferno. The firemen had to put out the fire caused by the bombs. I know that the Lord was always beside us.

The sirens warn us of possible attack. Sometimes there were false alarms, but if we heard six sirens, we knew it was the real thing.

One time I was returning home and a siren warned of a legitimate attack. I witnessed a plane flying very low right above me and it was firing off a lot of artillery and its fire surrounded me. But not know just what to do and once again, I was saved. I ran to the bomb shelter where I fainted in my mother's arms. This was just one of the countless close calls that I experienced during the war.

The Italian army felt defeated due to lack of leadership, food and medical supplies. Allies from Britain and America flew over us and dropped messages advising us not to give up because they would be supplying us with food and medical needs. Children abandoned in the streets stole fruit from the stands and threw it at the Nazis. They are the ones who helped start the Civil War and push out the Nazis.

We were warned by the Americans to remain in our bomb shelters for our own safety. This was called "the four days in Naples. "during this time were in our shelter, everything was still, and we were very frightened. Suddenly everything was finally over. We came outside and we kissed the ground. We were alive. The whole thing was an awful nightmare. Then a wonderful thing happened; for the very first time, I was amazed back to see American soldiers entering Naples. I saw them in groups, in army trucks and jeeps everywhere. The soldiers gave us candy and chewing gum. The children were shouting, hey" G.I. Joe. Give me some chocolate and cigarettes". the soldiers all appeared handsome. Some were tall and blond. They looked great in their uniforms. I was so happy; I cannot believe the war was over. Everyone was celebrating with wine: friendly and thankful to God. The Allies landed in Salerno, and Monte Cassino, which was a battlefield. The Americans fulfilled their promise of bringing supplies for Italy.

5

My Life Takes an Unexpected Turn

Now, with the war over we were notified that my brother Salvatore was missing in action. Then we found out that, through the help of farmers, he was alive and safe. Finally, on his return home, my parents failed to recognize him as he had changed so much. He had a mustache and beard. My father screamed, "My son, my son you're alive!" when she finally realized it was Salvatore, my mom was so overcome in the emotional as were the rest of us. We all braced and happy tears, watched my father's face looking at the sky. He was so grateful to God for this moment.

The allies were still here in Italy and would be for quite some time. It would take years to before things where returned to normal. There was so much destruction. We all had a lot of patience, due to the necessities that were but lacking. Every day mother's offered their daughters to allies in exchange for food. Years later, it was easy to see how many children were born to these girls who had American partners of different race.

The times were difficult and as the days passed by I realized I had to get a job so I would be able to help my parents. I was fortunate to get work at a dry cleaners and laundry that was in the center of Naples. My work was altering uniforms that belong to the American soldier. Many of the customers were from Texas and they did a lot of singing in their own Texas style. My mom would prepare a lunch for my father and me, and he would stop at the cleaners every Wednesday and the two of us would enjoy lunch together. This was every Wednesday because my father attended Mass at the church across the street from where I worked. The business closed and the Americans were transferred elsewhere.

We found out that Allies opened a quartermaster store in a village called Secondigliano, near Naples. They repaired shoes, tailoring and other work which was performed by the Italian and German prisoners. As I was not of a job, my grandmother Caterina, and I talked to the captain in charge. We filed our applications. We were interrogated by the Office and advised to wait outside until he reached the decision. While waiting, I noticed a small group of American soldiers conversing in a corner. There were not aware of us at all. Like a magnet, my eyes were focused on the one blond in the group. I felt something very special about him. I was fascinated by his strong looking build and I felt this man must have blue eyes. It seems strange but true, I would strongly drawn to this soldier from America.

We got good news, we were hired. My mom would be very pleased to hear about this. I hadn't bought called Zia Michela, living in a village, who was also hired their. I was very pleased with the work they hired me to do. I was sewing on machine and was happy with what I accomplished while employed there. There was an American lieutenant attached to me. He continually made a nuisance of himself, because I refuse to accept his offers of a date. He had a mean disposition which worked at times. I was worried I might lose my job. Finally his superiors received complaints from the workers about him. Then he was transferred.

While working on my machine there was a commotion down the other side of the room. An American staff sergeant was standing on the table and explaining in the best Italian he could for everyone to be honest and loyal workers. When I reached the area, there was my blond American that I had noticed some time previously and yes, he had blue eyes. Also now that he was head of tailoring which was my department, he was now my boss. All the Italians that were working liked him. He was very nice and he could speak our language, even though not perfectly. At lunch time we sat over to the side against a wall, he joined me. We became friends and I found myself giving him my lunch. He greatly enjoyed it because it was prepared Italian style. Once in awhile, Tony and his colleague Joseph Gentile would join me at lunch time. Joe called me the princess because I was always shy around these strange newcomers to my country. The staff sergeant, whose name was Tony Lamorte asked me to direct him to an Italian designer and patter, He was interested and he wanted to learn, while he was stationed at the base. He attended the class by Professor Scmonelli in Naples. We started to date and would travel around by jeeps and would sometimes stop at a pastry shop near where his class was held enjoyed sfoglitelle calde, a delicious and Italian pastry.

Tony's parents were Carmine and Anne Lamorte. They were both born in Potenza, Italy. They had three children, Anthony, John and Theresa, who were all born in East Boston, Mass. Anthony was born on February 22nd 1921. He attended schools in Boston. At the age of 18, the family sold their home and moved into the Bronx New York. In 1937, Tony found work at a tailor's in New York City. On December 26th 1941, Tony went into the army and arrived for basic training at a New Jersey camp. From there he went to camp Lee in Virginia, where he remained for three months. Then he was sent to North Africa in Oran, Morocco.

While he was stationed there in Oran, one day he met a French Moroccan. They started to date and from time to time went out dancing. But there was no time and they shipped out to Naples Italy. He did not see her for a while until the return on leave, where he surprised her and found her with another man. This of course ended their relationship.

Our courtship continued for awhile, we were very attached to each other from the beginning. We realized we were meant for each other. Tony wrote a letter to his parents in America and told them he found the girl of his dreams. Sunday he expected to marry her and wanted their blessing. Her name was Maria and she was a native of Naples Italy. They were very much in love and tried to see much of each other. They would go dancing in the camp and Tony would be so romantic, he would take her out in the horse and buggy. This made Maria very unsure of her feelings for Tony. He was born in America and she thought that this would only lasted a few days or weeks before he would leave for America and where would this leave Maria? But this was not the case. Tony asked her to marry him and Maria knew at that moment he truly loved her.

We kept seeing more and more each other and I remember it was turning to summer and the time where we celebrated the feast of St. Louis who in fact is my father's name day in Naples. My Mom and Dad wanted to see the man I was going to marry so I invited him to dinner. We all had a great time and they really liked him a lot and Tony like them to. He brought soap, cigarettes and meat, chocolate and other goodies. It was a beautiful day and we were very pleased and we knew that he was a good man and that we would be very happy. My dad was so proud of the work that he did that he showed Tony the picture of himself on the train. He had devoted all his life for his family. Tony was very impressed.

6

My Marriage to an American soldier

Soon after, Tony went to talk to the captain to get the necessary papers ready for the marriage. After months passed by, we finally were able to get married. We got the necessary papers, but there were still difficult times to go through. There were a number of things we had to do. First of all my family had to be investigated and made sure we were good people. Next, I had to undergo a full physical. We were going back and forth and everything was a big deal. They made it very difficult for Tony and I.

In the end, I was beginning to lose patience. Finally, all the paperwork was in order and the commander gave his OK. Tony's mother had sent a package from the United States containing a white satin wedding dress with lace detailing that she had made with her own hands. She had also sent a long veil of fine lace, a headpiece made of mother of pearl, White suede shoes, a ring and a three piece off white honeymoon outfit. The ring was most unusual, gold with rubies and rose details etched all around it. Everything seemed like a fantasy to me, as though I was dreaming it all.

On December 8th 1945 the day of obligation (The Immaculate Conception) We exchanged wedding vows. The wedding was held at St. Michael's in Naples, the mass started at 11:00 a.m. The church was very cold because all windows were still broken from the bombing. My dad looked like a million dollars but he was very nervous and shivering from the cold and his feelings were about his only daughter getting married. My mother looked very elegant, but was also very nervous but very moved because she probably was thinking that I would be leaving soon. My brother was also there and my uncle, cousins and friends.

We were all waiting for Tony and beginning to wonder where he was. I was really nervous. He was already half an hour late. You could hear people wondering out loud. All the sudden, entry way of the church, Tony appeared with his captain, his best man, his friend Joe and other American friends. Tony was in his staff sergeant uniform and looked so handsome. To people married us an Italian priest and an English chaplain. The ceremony was beautiful. We were very lucky because a couple of Tony's friends had cameras and took several pictures, so we have memories of the event. When it was over, we walked towards the back of the church. Before we left the church, my brother came up to us and kissed me tenderly. Then he looks straight into my husband's eyes and said, "take care of my sister".

Outside a crowd had gathered. They were curious at this wedding between an Italian and an American. They waited to see us leave the church. Tony and I climbed into the jeep and went back to my parents' apartment house, where my parents had set up a surprise wedding feast in an empty apartment above theirs. We had champagne, liquors and cookies. Some of Tony's friend had made a three tier wedding cake and brought it as a surprise as well as ice cream. It was one of the happiest days of my life.

7

The Honeymoon

At 7:00 in the evening, I changed out of my wedding outfit into a two piece gray suit. Tony told me that we're going somewhere but he didn't tell me where, you was to be another surprise. He took me to Zia Theresa, our favorite waterfront restaurant. Their specialty was fresh fish, which they caught right there at the restaurant. The food was incredible. We ate, sitting close together, looking into each other's eyes. It was so romantic.

We spent that night at the house of a couple we knew, who had offered us their own bed for wedding night. They had fixed up the dead beautifully with fresh white linen. The following morning, they surprised us by knocking at the door and waking us up with a pot of hot chocolate. What they were really interested in, though, was an Old Italian custom of making sure that the new bride was a virgin for her wedding night. Curiosity killed the cat..... .

The next morning, we left for our honeymoon. We first set off by train for a few days in Rome, the eternal City. Then we returned to Naples, where we took a boat plane to Capri, the enchanted island. We visited the Church of St. Michael, the resort areas, the little steps leading up the steep hills, the narrow streets, too narrow for vehicles, and the tiny, colorful gift stores. The Blue grotto was closed so we couldn't go inside, but several years later I did go inside and it was breathtaking. This is where Clark Gable and Sophia Loren filmed the movie "it started in Naples".

We were so happy but our precious time together was slipping away. Soon Tony would have to come back to the base and return to his work and I would have to return to my parents' home.

8

My life changes in front of my eyes

As a war bride, I carried an American military PX identification pass with my photo on it at all times. With the past, I could buy food and shop at the Px. During this time, I lived with my parents and Tony lived on the base, but spent some time with me and my parents. Space was very tight because there were only two rooms and a bathroom. Once in awhile, Tony stayed overnight and we hung a current up to give ourselves a little privacy.

In March, three months after our marriage, I remember Tony was given 10 days special leave to visit his relatives in the province of Ripagandida, in the mountains of Potenza near Naples. I was very happy to visit them but I didn't feel too well on the trip. I felt tired and a little queasy. We visited Antonio and Felippo Spina, Tony's father's sister and brother-in-law. She noticed that I was looking pale and she pulled me aside. Quietly, she told me that was bothering me was only temporary, and that was a gift from God. At that point, I did not understand her and smiled weakly.

When I got home, I felt worse. I couldn't smell the coffee without feeling nauseous. Finally, I decided to get a medical checkup. Tony told me that I had the right to go to the Red Cross as an American war bride and I would get free care from them. The doctor was an American captain. After a complete examination, he said, "congratulations, you are three months pregnant. In November, you'll give birth to a baby". I couldn't believe everything that was happening to me but in my heart, I felt a deep joy when I accepted and understood the reality of becoming a mother myself. When I gave my parents to big news, they were overcome with emotion and their tears flowed.

Next thing I got letters from both the American and Italian Red Cross, informing me of a military regulation that required pregnant war brides to leave for the United States before they were six months pregnant. For me, I got the shock of my life because I was not expecting that I would have to leave so soon. It felt like a death sentence. For me it was very difficult because I would have to leave everything, including my husband who was still in the Army in Italy. Of course, he would follow later, but we had no idea when. I had to except this; there was nothing I could do about it. My heart was broken, but I had to go ahead with plans.

June 12th 1946 was the dreaded moment of departure, when I would leave my beloved country; I would be separated from my adored family, my dear brother, who are love so much and my cousins. I cannot even imagine the pain, the torment, and then I thought about it and started to understand, that this was only the beginning of the pain. I was five months pregnant, the ship Vucania was already at the dock. It was only available for a short time.

My husband had bought an accordion for me to bring to his sister as a gift from Italy. The time for departure had arrived. At that moment, I somehow got courage but it was not for me. It was something stronger than me. I believed that it came from the divine source. The Lord was with me, he gave me the strength to go on and I know he would never abandon me, even in my darkest moments.

I went on deck with the other war brides and was looking for my family through the portals. I wanted to give them the last kissed and the last goodbye. It was very stressful and I could see the boat was moving away. I saw my mother faint and when I saw that, I went away, because I could not handle the emotion of it all, and I fainted away too.

One of the Marine guards picked me up thinking that I have fainted because of my pregnancy. But it was because I was overcome with the emotional leaving my family. I was devastated at having to leave them. This was one of the saddest days in my life.

I didn't know immediately, but the boat had to stay in port for several days for quarantine, during this time, I heard my name being called. I thought I was dreaming. But then I saw a small rowboat and recognize my brother with another man in the boat with him. Then I recognized the man with him as my husband, Tony, dressed in one of my brother civilian suits. I had never seen him out of uniform, which is why didn't recognize him at first. They couldn't come on to the boat, so all I could do was wave to them and call out to them.

Also would broke my heart to leave my parents, still I was not worried about how they would live because of my first cousin, Salvatore the priest, and his sister, Chiaina, or right there to look after them. It took care of everything; getting their pensions and making sure they got their medications. They did so much for my parents.

9

I arrive in America

We were two or three days sitting there in the port, then the boat finally left and it took about 12 days to sail to the United States. The trip seemed very long because I missed everybody. I was very depressed and worried about what I would find when I arrived in the United States. I had no friends to come to and no known relatives. I tried to be happy, but I couldn't. I had no idea what will happen to me. Although I felt as though my heart was broken, still I felt that this was my destiny. Somehow I felt that I had to conquer these obstacles and I prayed for the Lord to give me guidance from his infinite bounty.

On the boat, I met a couple of women; Anna, who was going to Brooklyn; Rita, who was going to Staten Island; and another who was going to Texas. Rita's husband was a baker and we got together later.

Finally, we reached a United States and the boat passed by the Statue of liberty. I was very disappointed because the weather was drizzly and gray. We could hardly see the stature through the fog. I felt like crying and said to myself, "oh my God! I thought I was coming to the City of Gold, the Land of enchantment", because of what I've been told before I left Italy. Then the boat docked at pier 84 in New York City. It was June 12th 1946.

The Red Cross held my arm and helped me off the boat with all my baggage down the gangplank. My new mother-in-law sent me a coat so that she would recognize me when I landed. I was wearing the coat with a name tag. I looked around and felt as though I was in a dream. "Where am I?" I wondered, "What my doing here?" I stepped off the gangplank and my feet touched American soil I stood there feeling like a piece of baggage, like I didn't belong anywhere.

All the sudden, I felt my heart beating so fast. I recognize three people right in front of me. It was my new family. "It's them!" It was my husband's mother, father and sister waiting for me. They recognize the coat. It all happened so fast. We looked at each other and we all recognize to we were from pictures we had sent. They threw their arms around me. I felt overcome with emotion. These are strangers but there were my new family in America. Two other members of my new family had planned to meet me but couldn't be there. Tony's cousins Dan and Lina Lamorte, whose new baby boy, Robert, choose this day, June 12th 1945 to be born.

We got into the car and drove towards the Bronx, which was a beautiful village in those days. I was sitting in the car and looking all around. And I started to feel better about things. I was wearing a simple but elegant dress of pink and gray silk. You couldn't even see that I was pregnant because of the way the dress was made. My new family spoke Italian. I wasn't feeling so alone. They welcomed me with open arms and I felt more at home with each passing moment.

Everything looks so different from what I was used to in Italy. I was especially impressed with the fire escapes which had never seen before. It was just like looking at a Hollywood movie but this was real and right in front of my eyes. It took us almost an hour to get to the Bronx. Tony's family wanted to know all about their son who they had not seen for three years. So I told them, "Your son Tony was one of the lucky ones. Because he had the skill of tailoring, he didn't have to go to the front. One of the captains's selected him for his own personal Taylor. Don't expected him to look the way he did when he left he is a mature man now and he's fine. He will be discharged and come home soon". They were happy to hear all about their son.

We stopped right outside their three story apartment building. Tony's family lived at the top of the building, on the third floor. We went up the stairs and into the neighbor's apartment, next door. The neighbors were Maddalena and Antonio Mingoia and their four children, Charlie, Concetta, Anthony and Margarita, and the youngest, who I called "bambola Cinese—Chinese doll" because she looked just like a little Chinese doll. Concetta and my sister-in-law, Theresa was very close. Later Concetta married a very nice boy, Tommy Scalera. We used to all go out and socialize together.

Maddalena, a mother-in-law's neighbor, became like a mother to me. She taught me how to cook. I was very fond of her. My sister-in-law and I would visit her all the time. She was from Salerno, near Naples and would cook wonderfully. I would smell delicious food from the hallway. Her husband, Antonio, was also very big hearted and loved to speak Italian with me. He is to offer me his home made wind which was very strong. I wasn't used to such a strong wind, so I would take a few sips of it.

Maddalena had been sick and all the family was gathered in the apartment. We were invited in and couldn't believe my eyes. A long table was loaded with goodies, cakes and cookies of all kinds and of sweet things. I'd never seen such a thing. Someone told me to be careful about what I ate because of my pregnancy. She told me to watch my diet and not get fat. I asked her," What's that?" I explained that it wanted to enjoy all the blessings of America, because I had just experienced three years of war with not much food to eat. And I told of how difficult it had been. They were surprised to hear what I had gone through and they couldn't believe it.

My mouth was watering. Even my dreams I had never seen anything quite like the abundant food laid out on the table. I tasted a little of everything. I felt even more comfortable.

Time passed and I started to really miss my husband and my faraway family. But everyone was trying to make me feel better. Tony's brother, John only spoke a few words of Italian but he would joke with me. He had chestnut colored hair but looked a little like Tony in his face. His sister, Terry also looked like Tony. John would tell me that I had to learn English. He would joke with me and say, "Maria, when Tony comes home, you got to say him: You want chicken, you want to neck"? And I would ask, "What's a chicken? What's a neck"? John knew I was sad and he wanted to make me smile.

John was engaged to a girl named Maria, but they called her Tess. Her mother and father, Theresa and Nicola Di lucchio, were also Italian from Rionero, near Naples, so she could speak Italian. She was very attractive with black hair and was a year younger than me. We became very good friends. And her mother was very fond of me also.

Some time passed by and I was interested in everything new. It was the end of the summer and I was taken to see the big city of New York, the city that the whole world talks about. I stared at the skyscrapers. I especially wanted to see St. Patrick's cathedral. We went to see famous night clubs like the Copacabana, the famous radio City Music Hall, everything was spectacular and I was so impressed. It was like a dream come true. I enjoyed everything but I was in a kind of fog. I couldn't believe my eyes.

The only thing that was difficult for me was that I couldn't understand what people were saying and I couldn't speak the language. I did say a few words but not enough to have a conversation. What I was out in the car, I would look around at the words that I saw on the streets and tried to pronounce them, but it was tough. I learned little by little. I will listen to radio and go to movies and look at magazines to learn English.

My parents and my brother were always on my mind. Not one day passed without me thinking about the. Sometimes I would go in to my room and cry, because I missed them so much. I would have done anything to see them again, but my new family was my life now and I had to go foreword on a path I had chosen.

10

My Husband Comes Home

A month after I arrived in America, Tony finally came home. It was summer and hot so the screen door was open. He knocked on the apartment door and his mom saw him through the screen but didn't recognize him. "Who are you?" She asked. "Ma, it's me Tony, Your son." He said. He had changed. He'd matured. I was so happy to see him. It was one of the most beautiful days of my life. Now living was complete. Tony was finally home, I was soon to become a mother, and now I felt that through the Lord I had courage to overcome all obstacles.

His parents had a little gathering for Tony's homecoming, and all the friends and family came. Everybody was happy to see him back home.

It was the end of summer and the family was preparing for John and Tess's wedding in the early September. I felt like a balloon. I had gained so much weight that is a shame to go out. My clothes didn't fit me anymore, so Tony made me a new dress for the wedding. Unfortunately, it made things worse. The fabric had big flowers all over which made me look even worse than before, but had to wear for the wedding all the same. But never wore it again.

I remember that about this time, Tony wanted to give me a very special surprise. He arranged for me to talk on the telephone with my family in Italy. I was so happy to hear the voices of my faraway adored family, that I forgot the time and distance we talked about 24 minutes. The operator never told me about the time, so Bill was $85. Tony was so good to me that he never complained about the bill, but he sewed a jacket for someone to pay for the call.

My in-laws were good to me. My mother-in-law, Anna, was a beautiful woman with black hair. She and I got along pretty well. She was a night owl and liked to stay up late talking with me in the kitchen. This was hard for me because I was

26

used to going to bed early. My father-in-law, Carmine, was very handsome with wavy hair that turned white when he was young. He was a quiet man but very good natured. My sister-in-law, Terry, was a very beautiful girl with long, black hair that hung down her back. She was very intelligent and could play the accordion by year. She could also sing. Terry, Tony, and John, his brother, all resembled one another.

Tony found a job in the city and I found a job in a dry cleaning store. I tried my best even though I could not speak English yet been made a lot of mistakes, especially when I would write things down. I wanted to help with the money, because Tony and I were saving up so that we could buy our own place.

11

My Big Event

I was getting close to having my first baby, so I stopped working. It was November 16th and I was not feeling well. I was very heavy. My mother-in-law recommended an Italian doctor. He was supposed to be a specialist and she was sure that he was going to help me. She panicked when I didn't feel well and called my neighbor, Maddelena. The two women looked at each other. I didn't want go to the hospital, but the pain was becoming worse. They may be walk back and forth and then gave me a glass of cognac, which they said would make me feel better. I wanted something to eat.

Then, all the sudden, my water broke and I was bleeding a lot. It took me to the Catholic hospital, St. Joseph's in Yonkers, but the family was not allowed in with me. I was all alone again. No one spoke Italian and the doctor wasn't there. I rang the bell and of the nuns came in. I was desperate but she did understand what I was saying. I almost pulled her habit off. I was yelling for the doctor. She tried to make me come down and told me that the doctor was coming.

Finally, the doctor came. It was difficult because it was a dry birth and they had to use instruments to get the baby out. Because of this, the baby shoulder was dislocated during the birth. The nuns didn't believe in using any medications during birth, which made it very difficult and painful for me. On November 17th, at around 12:00 midnight, my beautiful baby daughter, Anna Marie, was finally born. She had a very little light colored hair like a father. The grandparents were full of joy because of their first grandchild and were both crazy about her. For them, she was a living doll. Tony's mother started selling little clothes for her. Later, when she started to learn to walk, Tony's mother would teacher had a dance the Neapolitan Tarantella.

I'd been in America for six months by now, but it was still tough for me. I couldn't get used to it yet but some invisible force drove me foreword. It was in winter that never seen so much snow in my whole life. In Italy, although we have the four seasons, it was very mild. If we ever had a few flakes of snow, it would melt before it hit the ground. It was unforgettable and very cold, but I loved it. I had never worn pants before, but for the first time in my life, I bought long slacks, boots and all the right clothing for cold weather. That puts it all on and felt like a child again. It was a fantastic feeling and I went out and rolled around in the snow, like a carefree kid. I felt a crazy sensation and the smell snow was in the air and it was extraordinary.

We still lived with my in-laws on 224th Street in the Bronx. We lived in one bed-room, but it was temporary. The baby was growing, she was about two or three years old, and I found a job in New York at Roger and Pete on Madison Avenue. They made men's wear and I worked as a seamstress there. Meanwhile, my mother-in-law babysat for our daughter.

Every morning, I would leave with Tony for the train to New York. One day, it happened that in the crowd on the train, we got separated. Tony got off, but I could even get to the door and I had Tony's lunch sandwich. I was scared and felt all alone. I couldn't speak English well yet, so I yelled out, "Tony, a maren." which is Neapolitan for sandwich. He told me to get off the next Asian and wait there for him. This was a terrifying experience for me. But all turned out all right in the end.

12

The Next Few Years

My daughter, little Anna Marie, was growing up healthy and happy. She drew people to her. After three years, I found out that I was pregnant again. Everything was going well. This time, I went to a German doctor who warned me to watch my weight. He told me not eat salt and avoid complications. During this pregnancy, I only gained 18 lbs. While I was pregnant, my mother-in-law visited Italy with her daughter, Terry. When she came back, she became sick. I was eight months pregnant and I would help her and try and make her feel better.

We had moved to our own home on O'Neal place in the Bronx and brought our first Philco television and some furniture. My husband was hoping for a boy, but for the second time, he picked up a beautiful baby girl, Carmine, with black hair that looks like velvet, blue eyes and rosy cheeks. The nurses put a blue ribbon in her hair. This time Tony was with me for the birth.

Meantime, Tony's mother was getting worse. She was happy though that the new baby, Carmine, resembled her. She wanted to see the baby often. In her heart, she knew that she was near the end of her life. She was getting worse and worse. Finally, we took her to Lenox Hill Hospital, where it found out that she had the horrible disease of leukemia, a cruel destiny. When, Carmine was five months old, her grandmother died. She was only 47 years old, leaving everybody who loved her devastated by her death.

My husband was devastated by the death of his mother because she loved her so much. It was a very emotional time for us all. We made arrangements for her funeral. My husband wanted our oldest daughter, Anna Marie, who was about three years old, to see her grandmother laid out. I did not approve of the idea, but he really wanted her to be there because she had been so close to grandmother. When she saw her grandmother lying there, she was surprised and said, "Oh, why is grandma's sleeping with all her clothes on?" because my husband did not want to leave his father alone, we decided to move back in with him. I sold all the furniture we had and went back to live with my father-in-law, still in the Bronx.

Time went by and it was now 1950. Tony realized that I was really homesick and decided that I should go home to see my family in my native country. It was good timing because my one and only brother was going to get married.

I went to Italy by boat with my two young children, ages 1 and 4. When we got to Italy, it was very difficult because they both got very sick. They were allergic to the milk or some food and both developed skin rashes, one on the head and the other on her face. I wired Tony, who sent some extra money which I used to take the children to a specialist, who gave them penicillin which cleared up the problem.

The wedding was very nice. The bride, Maria, was also from Naples and my brother seemed happy. They had four children, and Gino, Patricia, Dario, and John Luka.

My little daughter was taken care of by my mother and father because they loved her so much. She was like having a living doll. When we left, my parents were broken hearted because they love the little one so much. A big memory of her was left in their hearts.

13

My Children Start to Grow Up

My daughter learned to speak Napolitano by playing with the kids outside. When she got back, my husband and my sister-in-law were surprised because Anna Marie would reply to them in Neapolitan dialect.

Our daughters were both cute and lively and were growing up. They started to go to kindergarten and elementary school, at Lady of Grace in the Bronx. The school was just one block away from where we lived. The older one, who was very capable, would sometimes take care of the younger crossing the road to school. I was not worried about them because I would watch them from the window.

The days passed by with regular rhythm. It was New Year's Eve and we were invited out to party. We met all our friends and spent a beautiful night. We drank all little more than usual and were feeling very mellow. The result was apparent eight months later, when I delivered a baby boy. Unfortunately I had had a cesarean and it was a very difficult birth. Two specialists add to assist with the birth. Luckily the baby was beautiful and healthy with blue eyes and jet black hair. With the help of the Lord, I and my son both made it, but it was a miracle. My husband was very happy with the sun that he had always wanted. We called him Anthony Michael Lamorte.

My oldest daughter was so good; I never had to worry about her. If I had to be gone, she would watch over the two younger children like a mother and I could trust her completely. When they were all older, we would go on vacation and have a lot of fun. We would call them the three musketeers.

Little by little, I would try to learn English, through movies and magazines. I tried to go to night school and learned the grammar, but they would say that I didn't need it because my conversation was so good. I used to help the children with their homework and encourage them with their schoolwork.

My sister-in-law, Theresa, got married on April 22nd, 1951 to Di Lucchio, a tall and very handsome man. They moved out from my father-in-law's apartment. We were still living there but had three children now and decided to leave the paternal House and the Bronx and wanted to buy a nice little home for ourselves. We also wanted Tony's father to come and live with us. He liked the idea and wanted to help us financially.

We found a nice slow House at 1204 Adee Avenue in the Bronx. We lived right across from a project with a park. There was a short cut for the children through the park to their school, St. Filippo and Jemes. I would volunteer for the school and look after the children while they played outside during the lunch time. One day, Carmen (who we now call Connie) came home from school hiding something in her jacket. "look what I've got Ma!" she shouted excitedly. It was a puppy: a tiny, puffy, black and white ball of fur. He was so young and frightened that we put him in a box with a clock so that the ticking would seem like his mother's heart. One of Connie's school friends had given him to her. We decided to call the puppy quotes "lucky". All the children love him, especially my son, Anthony who would take him out on the weekends. Also I wasn't expecting to have a dog, somehow lucky became like a child to me. He lived for 18 years and when he finally died, I missed him so much, just like a person.

I wanted to a lot more and so I learned how to drive a car. When I went for the test the first time, I was asked this question: what to you do when you see a cattle crossing? "What's a cattle?" I asked. I was told home and study the books and more. The second time I passed and I was so happy. Now I had more freedom.

At this time, Tony was traveling a lot for his company and I would be the car. He would stay away couple of days once in awhile and I would be anxious waiting till he returned. We were lucky because we got a good deal on a car through his company. We were able to buy a used Cadillac at a very good price.

The children were growing up, Anna Marie was sweet 16, Connie was 13 and Anthony was 8. We had a little party for Emery with her friends. My sister-in-law had two beautiful children by this time. The daughter, Adriana, was blond and beautiful, the son, Nicola, was named for his grandfather.

My father-in-law, Carmine, was working in an iron works. After eight long years loneliness since his wife, Tony's mother, had died, Carmine finally found happiness again with Maria, a woman who he met at his workplace. He and Maria got married and moved in with her into her home and there were very happy together. We would sometimes go and have meals with them.

14

We Move On

Times were changing and we decided that it was time to move on to do something better for the family. We looked in the Port Chester/Rye area and found a beautiful, elegant house on King Street in Port Chester. The House had full sun and it was spacious, everyone had their own Room. We were on the same block as Tony's brother, John, in one house and his sister, Theresa in another. John had married Angelo Di Lucchio's sister, Tessy Di Lucchio. John and Tessy and had two beautiful children, Joan and Carmine, named for his grandfather, but later became known as John John.

The cousins were all friends and would go out together. Anna Marie was one year older than Joan. Tony was quite strict with the girls, more Italian, I was more easily with them, more American. They were already growing up. Anna Marie was going to her first year of college and had bought her own car. One time, the three girls wanted to talk to a movie together but Tony didn't want them to. Finally, Jones' mother, Tessy persuaded him to let them go.

They went to the movie in Anna Marie's car. On the way home, they took a shortcut through a very expensive residential area and got a flat tire. The didn't know what to do and were frightened in the dark. In the distance, they heard a coyote howling. Finally decided to gather their courage and holding hands, when up to the gate of an estate. Inside the people were dancing and having a party. The girls were scared to go when but decided to ring the bell. The people inside were very understanding of the girls dilemma and let them come inside and use the telephone to call home. When the girls left, they put a dime on the table for the phone call. Tony did want to believe the story until he saw the tire. The girls had to prove what had happened.

My niece, and Joan, became a good singer and she appeared in a few shows. She was also in a singing contest with Domnico Madugno and won second prize. Joan had met Jim Lauro when she was a young girl and a decided to get married. They had a beautiful wedding and Joan looked radiant. Later they had two children, Gina and Jimmy.

Carmine was in high school. Sometimes I would takers school, other times she would take the bus. My son, Anthony Jr., but was going to elementary school at Rye, and he could walk to school. He made friends with a bully in school called Anthony Tristucci, a good boy who lived in our neighborhood and they used to go to school together. Bois

My daughter Carmen was also called Connie. She was growing up a very beautiful girl, but I was always worried about her. She was quite introverted it wouldn't confide in me. She also had a mind of her own. She was now almost 18 years old and had a calendar in room and was crossing out each day on it. At the time I didn't realize what was going on. The two sisters would go to Newark together and meet this guy Mike Taylor, who worked in New York. Through him, Connie met Tom Brady.

Once in awhile, Connie would bring, home so we could get to know him. My husband Tony was always in different to him and treated him very coldly. Tom was an affectionate died when he was 17 he had left home in Tennessee and had enrolled in the Marines. My husband was so concerned about the situation and did what Connie to see the guy again, so he made Connie swear on the Bible that she would see Tom anymore. Connie put her hand on the Bible and swore, but she didn't mean it.

While this was going on, I didn't feel good. I was worried about my health; so I went for a checkup and had an X-ray. The doctors concluded that I needed a hysterectomy. Thank you God, for always being with me and everything was all right. There were no complications. I stay several days in hospital, and then I was home convalescing. Connie would call home from school early and would help with housework. Slowly, everything returned to normal.

Tony decided to take the whole family on vacation to Italy. We all got vaccinated and got our passports, including Connie. It was late afternoon, and my daughter Connie had not come home from school. Anna Marie came in and saw how worried I was. "What happened? Where is your sister? Why hasn't he come home from school?" I asked her. Anna Marie offer excuses for Connie. He was getting dark and we didn't know what to do. All the sudden, I got an idea. I dropped everything and ran upstairs to Connie's room and looked in her closet. I saw that lots of stuff was missing.

Now I understood why she had been marking off her calendar. I wanted to scream and cry; it felt as though my hair was standing on end and as though night was falling, slow and sad; I thought I was going to die from the pain. I didn't know what to do. I thought that she had run away with this fellow, but this thought was impossible to accept. I called my in-laws next door and they comforted me. Tony and I lay together on the bed, crying like to babies and clinging to each other. We could understand what had happened. We were looking for answers but couldn't find them. Our little girl had gone away. She was just 18.

Next morning, the phone rang. It was my adored daughter, my baby. "Mama, forgive me! It was only an impulse. I'm OK. We got married in Colorado with a justice of the peace. Mama, I didn't do anything wrong. Give me your blessing. I hope that Daddy will forgive me for what I did. We love each other very much and we're happy". Tony and I felt chills run up and down. But as long as they were all right, we were relieved. My heart ached!

It was 1967 and even though we were soon due to go to Italy on vacation, we insisted that they return and have a church wedding in the eyes of God. We had to hurry up like crazy. We did everything possible. In two weeks, I bought a wedding gown, wrote invitations, arranged for the wedding. They got married in Corpus Christi Church in Port Chester, New York. Connie wore a wedding dress made out of designs like a Spanish Gown and was very fashionable. Her eyes were only for Tom, she was in love with him. The ceremony took place at 5:00 in the afternoon. The reception took place at Rye Ridge Club. Anna Marie was the maid of honor, Anthony was ushering. Everything turned out beautifully and we accepted Tom into our own family.

Finally we were ready to leave for the trip to Italy, but the evening I had been through, I came down with roseola. I was praying for a quick recovery. I went to the doctor and found out that my nervous system was upset. Luckily, I did have a quick recovery and we were able to leave on the trip. We were also happy that my daughter was settled in her marriage but she would not be coming with us. She stayed with husband in Monticello, N.Y. who was working as an undercover agent in a resort. A. Gorman and her husband were also singing at that time. Tom was acting as a decoy in the restaurant by playing the role of a maitre d.

Anna Marie came with us on the trip and she missed her sister. Anthony, our son, wanted to bring his friend, Vincent, with us, so we brought him too. We had the best time; we went to visit my mother and father and took them to the hotel the Vesuvio in Naples. My parents were so happy to see their grandchildren. We visited Rome, and Capri. People thought my daughter and I were sisters.

We also went to visit my first cousin, Salvatore Salerno, the priest, after so many years of not seeing him. He performed Mass, then we went to his sister Shirley is House and she had made a beautiful cake for our son's birthday. The whole visit was unforgettable and everyone had a good time. While we were there, Anna Marie's friend, Mike Taylor, called her from America. My husband and I were confused because we felt that he was not good enough for our daughter, which is the reason we took her with us to Italy.

15

Anna Marie's Wedding

Anna Marie had completed two years of college and was going to continue, but she had seen her sister and cousin get married into became frightened of becoming an old maid. Choose a beautiful woman, but she did understand what can happen in life. In her head, she was anxious and she thought that life was passing her by and so she decided she wanted to get married to Mike. They got engaged.

My husband and I were not enthusiastic about this marriage but there's nothing we could do, they had made up their minds. They said a date and prepared for the wedding. It happened on September 28th 1968 in Port Chester, N.Y. at Corpus Christi Church.

She wore a beautiful dress made of sand with lace and pearls and a long train. She looked so elegant. Mike was English and made a nice couple. I hope they would be happy. Her maid of honor was Dominica, a close girl friend. Connie was one of the bridesmaids. Anthony was one of the ushers with another girl. Mike's brother, Gregory, was best man.

The reception was in that Tardy Place in the Bronx. Tony had made me a beautiful blue dress for a reception. It had ostrich feathers around the hem. I family were little out of hand. Then, the couple left for their honeymoon in Bermuda. I thank the Lord that my two daughters were settled down but little did I know what was going to happen. You never know what life will present you.

It turned out that Mike had to be given oxygen on the flight to Bermuda. They thought the he was having a heart attack, but he was really suffering from the effects of the wedding libations!

16

We Move to Connecticut

After Emery got married, we moved to Connecticut which I had always liked. Before deciding to move there, we had visited Jenny and Al D'Amato often in Fairfield. We had met them through Tony's work. The D'Amato's had a log cabin on the beach at that time and would invite us up to eat with them, and Jenny was a very good cook and made delicious meals. They had a dress factory in Bridgeport and Tony would bring them work. We got very close and people thought Jenny and I were sisters, since we looked a lot alike. We would also go on cruise vacations with them. One time we all went to Morocco, Spain and then visited North Africa and Casablanca together.

Jenny and Al had three children: Philomena, Matthew and Joanna. Matthew became our son Anthony's godfather and Joanna was the same age as Connie and became very close friends with her.

We found a house in Fairfield, but couldn't move in until October. Anthony was still in school, which started in September. Al D'Amato sister, Nancy, offered to have Anthony stay with them for the month of September, so he wouldn't miss any school. They're very kind to him and took great care of him, making sure that he did his homework each day. He called her Zizzy.

Our son, Anthony, was the last one home with us. He liked living in Fairfield and was so happy to be able to walk down the road to Roger Ludlow high school. I was in love with this cute little house. It had less space than all the others we have lived in, it was sunny and was a blessed home for us. I felt something special in my heart because from every window in the House I could hear the whistle of the trains, which ran in back of the House to the nearby station and reminded me of the beautiful whistle of my childhood. I felt that God had given me this special reminder of my dear father, who always seems to be here with me.

Anthony had dream to become the best fencer and his dream came true. At as high school there was a fencing school, Mr. Moore, and a good fencing team. Anthony was left-handed and when he was home, he would practice by himself in addition to all the school practice. Before the time he had finished school, he became captain of the team and had won many trophies in competition with fencers from all over the country. He won first place in the Connecticut fencing championship. He also like tennis and became a tennis captain and he also played soccer. Today, his house is full of fencing trophies.

I decided that I needed to get some exercise. The YMCA was nearby, within walking distance of the House, so I started to swim regularly there. One day, I was swimming and I met Helen Hudok, who was there for swimming therapy because she had an accident which had injured her neck. She was wearing a neck brace. We became good friends and are still Friends today. In the YMCA exercise room, I made another friend, Rosa Mauro, a fellow Italian, who is still a friend. She is now a widow and I take her shopping sometimes because her eyesight is not too good.

Our next-door neighbors, Maureen and George Champagne became friends to and we spend a lot of time together, picnicking and enjoying meals at our house. Maureen was originally from England. Even though they had difficulties in their marriage and got divorced and have moved away, Maureen and I are still friends.

One day I was shopping in the store and started to talk to young lady. I found out that her husband used to live in the Bronx near one of my husband's relatives. There names were Gino and Marie Massafra and we became friendly with them also.

Ethel and John Burns were neighbors of Paula Scalzi, the mother of Gary, Anthony's best school friend. We got friendly and would see each other once in awhile. Ethel helped me with writing the story in the beginning and wrote out a few pages of the story for me by hand. Then Ethel couldn't help me out anymore because she got sick.

17

Our Children, The Third Generation

One year had passed already and we missed our daughter, Connie. She had moved to Port Chester N.Y. from Monticello. We found out that she was in the family way. We all were so very happy at the thought of becoming grandparents and my children become aunt and uncle. We were eagerly awaiting exciting event. Patricia Brady arrived in September 1969. She was a beautiful baby with velvet black hair and blue eyes, rosy cheeks like to apples. The nurse put a blue bow in her hair. She was a living doll.

At this time, I was working, but I would leave my job for clock each afternoon, and drive all the way the Port Chester on high way to see my jewel, my grand-daughter. What Patricia was baptized, my daughter and son became her godpar-ents'.

The children surprised us with a party in Westport for our 25th wedding anni-versary, December 8th 1970. They put an announcement in the local paper with details about my life story and a photograph of me and Tony. They invited all our relatives and friends from the Bronx and Port Chester, as well as Fairfield. For me, it was a total surprise. They told me that we were going to the opera, so I was all dressed up in a special dress. I will never forget that day.

After some time, Connie and her family moved to Connecticut next door my niece, Joan. Connie's second child, Tom Brady, was born in Connecticut. He was also a beautiful baby with blond hair and blue eyes. When they saw him, everyone exclaimed that he looked like his grandfather, Anthony Lamorte.

Meanwhile, Connie's husband, Tom Brady, was a private investigator and his work was very dangerous. One time he got hit in the head with the end of a shotgun. But he wanted to better himself and make a life for himself and his family in Tennessee, where he had been raised. All this family was there and then his mother had given him some land. He wanted to build a house on it. My daughter did not want to move.

They had been Tennessee for two months, Patricia was two years old and Tommy was 18 months old. We found out that Emery was pregnant again. We're preparing for Thanksgiving. The night before, we were downstairs watching teepee. All of a sudden it was 10:00 in the evening and the telephone rang. My husband and my son were looking at each other. It was bad news. My daughter's husband had been in a car accident in Tennessee. We were told that he had been taken to the hospital but he was already dead by the time the phone rang. My daughter needed us. We were all in a state of shock.

The next morning Tony, my son and I all flew to Tennessee. When we saw our daughter, she was not herself; she was in a state of shock. She had no strength in did not want to believe that her husband was dead. She didn't cry but held everything inside. She would faint all the time. Tom's cousin, Curtis, had been in the car with him. It was a miracle that he was saved but he was badly injured. My husband, Tony, had to go to identify the body.

Funeral arrangements had to be made. My daughter gave all her possessions away to the Tennessee relatives and planned to move back to Connecticut with her children. For my daughter, Connie, her world had crumbled. We brought her back to Fairfield with us.

Tony and I suggested that she take a trip; go to Italy, anything to get her mind of the tragedy. But she did what do anything. While she was living with us, Tom's cousin Curtis came to visit her several times. She was so lonely and Curtis must have reminded her of her husband, Tom. Anyway, they ended up getting married and bought a house and a car. Curtis even started a business as a carpet contractor in Fairfield. When I found out they were going to move to Arizona, I was broken hearted, because I new I would miss the children so much. There were my first grandchildren and after they left, I started to replace them with food and gained a lot of weight.

I couldn't stay away from them, so it went to visit the family in Arizona, where we found out that Connie was pregnant with her third child. Patty and Tommy had started school there and would write us letters about how they missed us. Connie second son, Albert was born in late January. I flew out there be with them when he was born.

Connie's marriage was not working out, so she decided to leave Curtis and return to Connecticut. She and the children found an apartment near us and I was so happy that my grandchildren around again. There were growing up and were happy to be back in school here again. After a while, Connie met the right man for her. Craig Jones was an old friend of both, and Curtis and he had always admired Connie. Craig and Connie are still happily married today.

When she first married, Anna Marie lived in Brooklyn, New York. While she was living there, she had a son, a nice little blond boy, who was baptized Lawrence Taylor. As a little baby, he was very colicky. I stayed with her for one week and we were up night and day. Then I had to come back home. With the car and I felt very sad leaving her alone. While I was leaving, I was crying. Then I remembered the proverb that says that the mother bird has to let the baby birds leave the nest. And I knew that I had to let my daughter's fend for themselves for their own growth. I knew that God would watch over her and her baby.

A few weeks after Tom's death, Anna Marie gave birth to a beautiful daughter, who later looked like a little English girl with blond hair. It baptized her Victoria Taylor. This baby was the opposite of her brother, very quiet and very peaceful.

Later Anna Marie and Mike moved to Meriden, Connecticut to be near to us. They bought a condo and then years later bought a new house.

The destiny of my daughter, Anna Marie, was also cruel. She had to very young children by her husband had a drinking problem, which caused difficulties in their marriage and they fought. It was not his fault, but my daughter went through so much suffering in her marriage, because she was alone and had to work and take care of the children.

After 14 years of hell, she decided that enough was enough. She called Veterans Hospital, who came to get him and took Mike to the hospital. It was tough for both of them. After time in hospital, with the help of the Lord, he sobered up.

But my daughter had made up her mind, she decided she did not want to live with him anymore and filed for divorce. Today, the children are grown and have a good relationship with their father, who has remarried.

Later, and really met a fellow named Ray through a friend. He is a good person, very down to earth. He is a Mason and works and construction. When we need help, he is there for us and he has helped all the family with jobs a round of the houses.

Anthony and his friend Gary graduated together from Roger Ludlow high school with good grades. Anthony had his own car and loved to drive around in it. He wanted allowed on its own a decided to go to college at Miami University of Florida rather than Fairfield University here in Connecticut. He had made up his mind. He was going too far away from us and I was very upset about it. I had never thought he would leave us. He got himself a studio apartment in Florida but I worry about him. My thoughts were always with him and I would pray to God to watch over and bless him. He was my baby.

And he graduated from Miami University with a degree of bachelor of Science and Education and stayed in Florida. He maintained his interest in fencing and, after a while, and a fencing class, he met a beautiful blonde girl named Maggie. She was a law student, studying to become a lawyer. She came from a good family. Her parents were Alberto and Maria and her brother's name was Louis. He married Yanire and they're beautiful children are Adrian and Natalie.

They decided to get married and had two weddings, one in Florida on December 17, 1977 and one up here in the Connecticut. Tony and I went down to Florida for the wedding. Maggie became a lawyer and Anthony worked for the state of Florida as a placement specialist. They do not have their own children but spent a lot of time with their nephew and niece. In 1984, Anthony participated in the Olympics with the U.S. fencing team, as a helper.

When my grandchildren were growing up, I wouldn't invite them to come and visit with us for school vacations and to all go to nearby beach. Patty (Connie's first child), who grew up to be very beautiful, is still living in Connecticut. She is married and owns a gymnastics business with her husband, brother and sister-in-law.

My second grandchild, Anna Marie's first child, Lawrence, grew up to be handsome. One day he surprised us by eloping in getting married to a beautiful red haired girl named Heather. They live in Meriden, Conn. In 1997, Heather gave birth to my first great grandchild, Caitlin, or reminds me of myself when I was a child. She has blue eyes and red hair like a mother and his tall like a father. She is bright. Lawrence also called Larry, works in construction; he can do anything, especially in building around houses.

My third grandchild is Tom Brady, Connie second child. Thomas married to Judy, a childhood sweetheart who he met at school. Tom works with computers and they also live in Connecticut. Tom and Patty are very close. Tom and Judy had their first child, Kate, in 1997. She has beautiful golden hair like her mother. She is a living doll. Their second child was born in 2000 and is named Trisha. She had beautiful long black curly hair. She also is a living doll. Tom and Judy's third child was born in 2006 and they named him Thomas. He is very handsome and has dark hair.

The fourth grandchild is Victoria Taylor, called Vicki, Anna Marie's second child. Vicki is going to school for physical therapy here in Connecticut and she lives at home with her mother. Vicki looks like an English girl with a beautiful complexion. Vicki is engaged to a very nice man named Tony. Tony is a very hard worker and loves Vicki very much.

My fifth grandchild is Albert, Connie's third child. Years ago, with the help of God, Albert experienced a miracle. He was diagnosed with a brain tumor which was surgically removed. Today he is doing fine.

18

Deaths in the Family—Our Parents Pass On

It was December 8th 1970 when my dear daddy died. I couldn't get over to Italy to see him because there was not enough time to get there. In Italy, the body is kept for one day before burial, not like here in the states. I was overcome with grief at the thought that my father had gone.

So many unusual things happened on my father's death. He was very devoted to the Virgin Mary of the Immaculate Conception, which is celebrated as the day of obligation on December 8th. He wanted to die on that day and he did. Another unusual event was that while he was dying, he asked his niece Chirina to go to the church and light four candles. It so happened that he died at 4:00.

My daddy's faith was strong. He believed in the will of God. Through prayer he learned the secret of loving God and found himself at peace. He always felt the Holy Spirit within him.

Tony's father, my father-in-law, had been sick for quite awhile with an enlarged heart. On September 6, 1971, he also left this world. He was a good man and will always love him and missed him.

A year later, in 1972, my mother passed on. She had fallen in the House and broken her back. The doctor told her not to move. Because of complications from the accident, she got pneumonia and died. My brother called me and this time I went to Italy. Unfortunately, the plane was late on the trip over, which meant that I missed the bus at the other end. It was so mixed up. When I finally got to the House, I was very upset and not myself.

During my stay there, my father's body was dug up. In Italy, bodies are removed from the ground after two years and the bones are cleaned with alcohol and then stored in crypts. When my father's body was removed from the sand that surrounded it, I was amazed to see that the body was still intact. I couldn't believe that I was seeing my father's body. The skin was brown like tobacco leaves. I kissed him and it was something phenomenal that I will never forget as long as I live. It was an unforgettable experience for me.

19

The Epilogue

My husband, Tony has always been a good man. He is a dedicated and conscientious worker who gives his heart and soul to his job. Tony has worked in New York City for about 40 years. He has been with several companies; the last one is called Danny Michael, where he has worked for a number of years. The company is run by Frank Iorio, Sr. and his sons Frankie Jr. and Michael. Tony is production manager. Frankie Jr. is very fond of Tony and so are all the workers there. Anna Marie, the pattern maker, and several other have worked happily with him for years, too.

On the morning of February 22, 1998 he was surprised at work. It was his 77th birthday. He still went in to work. It was a normal day. As he walked towards his desk, one of his co-workers, Gigi, presented him with 24 yellow roses. Tony was so surprised. This was not all that was planned. Towards the end of the day, all of the employees got together and presented him with three big birthday cakes, while they were singing "Happy birthday to you". Then they gave him a birthday card, signed by everyone there, and tucked inside was a handful dollar bills. Tony was so surprised and overcome that his eyes filled with tears. When Tony leaves, he will be messed.

I was very upset because I wanted so much to write my story and find someone to help me. I prayed to the Lord for help and went to the Fairfield citizen News, the local Fairfield paper, and my prayers were answered.

The woman I talked to at the newspaper office was very understanding and told me that she had spoken to a woman who had just been in the office. This person would be perfect for what I wanted. She gave me a person's telephone number. I left the office, went to my car and found that I had a parking ticket. I was so upset and went to the police department to find out about it. They told me that I should not have parked where I did, but since it was the first time, I would not have to pay. I was so relieved.

When I got home, I had my husband called person, who turned out to be Patricia Ernest, a writer, who was able to help me with the rest of my story. Once again, my prayers were answered. We started to work together and I was very happy because the writing started to flow out how I wanted it.

On December 8, 1995, Tony and I celebrated our golden anniversary.50 years of marriage to one man. One of the biggest surprises of my life was to see my brother at the anniversary. My Children had arranged for my brother and his wife to come over to America. a few days before the actual anniversary, my grandchildren invited Tony and me to dinner for quality time together at Rocco's restaurant in Westport Conn. we arrived, expecting to see just the grandchildren. Instead, First Albert arrived with a movie camera and started taking movies. I was shocked because I didn't expect him. Then my daughter came in from Florida with her husband, then my son and his wife from Florida and finally, my older daughter arrived with her boyfriend Ray, bringing with them my brother and his wife from Italy. I couldn't believe my eyes, it was such a surprise to see them, right there in front of me.

For our anniversary, we got remarried at St. Thomas Aquinas, with Father Martino. My daughters, Connie and Anna Maria, sang and Craig played" Ave Maria" on the saxophone. The service was just for the family. Later, everyone met at Rose's family restaurant in Stratford, near the Sikorsky airfield for a party. It was a beautiful celebration and something I'll never forget.

Today, my first daughter, Anna Marie, has her own home in Meriden. She is divorced and never remarried. Beattie, her daughter, lives at home with her mom. Connie, my second daughter, remarried and is very happy with Craig Jones and they love each other. They live in Florida and their own home. Craig's parents, Walter and Fran Jones used to live in Stamford Conn. but have now sold their house and move down to Florida to and our friends of ours. My son, Anthony also lives in Florida, in Miami and is happily married with Maggie. They live full lives and are busy with their careers.

My existence has been a big dream; I've been through so many obstacles. The Lord gave me a beautiful family and most of all, my husband. We have always been together. With faith and trust we love each other. He has been all my life for without him, I would not have survived. We're happy and blessed.

I close this, my story with thanks to God who has always been there for me. At one time, I may have felt that life is one long search to know the meaning and purpose of my existence. However, now I know that my search is not about me, it is for God, who is the alpha and omega.

Maria's Mother, brother,
            father

Friends of the family

Salvatore at 25

First cousin
Padre Salerno
& His niece
Angela

May 1964

Maria at 4 yrs. old
& her brother Salvatore
at age 6.

Tony and Maria wedding
at church   1945

Maria and Tony in Capri

The after math
of WWII ruins.

Salvatore returing
home from the war

Sargent Lamorte seen
here working with the
Italians.

The wedding day 1945

Tony's army group

Tony, Maria's Mother and Maria

Maria and Husband and her
3 children, Ann Marie,
Connie, Anthony jr.

Maria and Tony

Maria, Tony and their
3 children growing
    up

Maria's 3 children
seen here together
and her oldest daughter
Ann Marie playing the
                        accordian

Here Maria and Tony are united with their son
Tony Jr. and Instructor Mr. Moore at a
Fencing Tournament (1975).

The five grandchildren: Patty, Larry, Vickie,
                         Tom, Dee

Anthonys trophy won in different tournments

Anthony my son fencing

Anthony my son in L.A. (olymic)

Olympic tournment in 1984 in L.A.

978-0-595-42289-0
0-595-42289-6

www.ingramcontent.com/pod-product-compliance
Lightning Source LLC
Chambersburg PA
CBHW022338290526
45785CB00017B/2102